Contents

Simple Slow Cooker Pork Roast

  4 **to 5 red potatoes, cut into bite-size pieces**
  4 **carrots, cut into bite-size pieces**
  1 **marinated pork loin roast (3 to 4 pounds)***
  ½ **cup water**
  1 **package (10 ounces) frozen baby peas**
  Salt and black pepper

*If marinated roast is unavailable, prepare marinade by mixing ¼ cup olive oil, 1 tablespoon minced garlic and 1½ tablespoons Italian seasoning. Place in large resealable food storage bag with pork roast. Marinate in refrigerator at least 2 hours or overnight.

1. Place potatoes, carrots and pork roast in **CROCK-POT®** slow cooker. (If necessary, cut roast in half to fit.) Add water. Cover; cook on **LOW 6 to 8 hours** or until vegetables are tender.

2. Add peas during last hour of cooking. Remove pork to cutting board. Cover loosely with foil; let stand 10 to 15 minutes. Season with salt and pepper. Slice and serve with vegetables.

makes 6 servings

Peach Cobbler

- **2 packages (16 ounces each) frozen peaches, thawed and drained**
- **¾ cup plus 1 tablespoon sugar, divided**
- **2 teaspoons ground cinnamon, divided**
- **½ teaspoon ground nutmeg**
- **¾ cup all-purpose flour**
- **6 tablespoons butter, cut into small pieces**
- **Whipped cream (optional)**

1. Combine peaches, ¾ cup sugar, 1½ teaspoons cinnamon and nutmeg in medium bowl. Transfer to 4½-quart **CROCK-POT®** slow cooker.

2. For topping, combine flour, remaining 1 tablespoon sugar and remaining ½ teaspoon cinnamon in small bowl. Cut in butter with pastry blender or two knives until mixture resembles coarse crumbs. Sprinkle over peach mixture. Cover; cook on **HIGH 2 hours.** Serve with whipped cream, if desired.

makes 4 to 6 servings

Tip: To make cleanup easier when cooking sticky or sugary foods, coat the inside of the **CROCK-POT®** slow cooker with nonstick cooking spray before adding ingredients.

Pesto Rice and Beans

1 can (about 15 ounces) Great Northern beans, rinsed and drained
1 can (about 14 ounces) chicken broth
¾ cup uncooked converted long grain rice
1½ cups frozen cut green beans, thawed and drained
½ cup prepared pesto
Grated Parmesan cheese (optional)

1. Combine Great Northern beans, broth and rice in **CROCK-POT®** slow cooker. Cover; cook on **LOW 2 hours.**

2. Stir in green beans. Cover; cook 1 hour or until rice and beans are tender.

3. Turn off heat; remove stoneware to heatproof surface. Stir in pesto and Parmesan cheese, if desired. Let stand, covered, 5 minutes or until cheese is melted. Serve immediately.

makes 8 servings

Easy Cheesy BBQ Chicken

> 6 boneless, skinless chicken breasts (about 1½ pounds)
> 1 bottle (26 ounces) barbecue sauce
> 6 slices cooked bacon
> 6 slices Swiss cheese

1. Place chicken in **CROCK-POT**® slow cooker. Cover with barbecue sauce. Cover; cook on **LOW 8 to 9 hours.** (If sauce becomes too thick during cooking, add a little water.)

2. Before serving, cut bacon slices in half. Place 2 pieces cooked bacon on each chicken breast in **CROCK-POT**® slow cooker. Top each chicken breast with 1 slice cheese. Turn **CROCK-POT**® slow cooker to HIGH. Cover; cook on **HIGH 10 minutes** or until cheese melts.

makes 6 servings

Corned Beef and Cabbage

> 1 head cabbage (about 1½ pounds), cut into 6 wedges
> 4 ounces baby carrots
> 1 corned beef (about 3 pounds)
>   with seasoning packet (perforate packet with knife tip)
> 4 cups water
> ⅓ cup prepared mustard
> ⅓ cup honey

1. Place cabbage and carrots in 4½-quart **CROCK-POT**® slow cooker. Place seasoning packet on top. Add corned beef, fat side up. Pour in water. Cover; cook on **LOW 10 hours.**

2. Remove and discard seasoning packet. Combine mustard and honey in small bowl. Slice beef; serve with vegetables and mustard sauce.

makes 6 servings

**EASY CHEESY
BBQ CHICKEN**

Simmered Napa Cabbage with Dried Apricots

4 cups Napa cabbage, cored and sliced thin

1 cup chopped dried apricots

¼ cup clover honey

2 tablespoons orange juice

½ cup dry red wine

Salt and black pepper

Grated orange peel (optional)

1. Combine cabbage and apricots in **CROCK-POT®** slow cooker. Toss to mix well.

2. Combine honey and orange juice in small bowl; mix until smooth. Drizzle over cabbage. Add wine. Cover; cook on **LOW 5 to 6 hours** or on **HIGH 2 to 3 hours** or until cabbage is tender.

3. Season with salt and pepper. Garnish with orange peel.

makes 4 servings

Barbecue Roast Beef

  2 **pounds boneless cooked roast beef**
  1 **bottle (12 ounces) barbecue sauce**
1½ **cups water**
10 **to 12 sandwich rolls, halved**

1. Combine roast beef, barbecue sauce and water in **CROCK-POT**® slow cooker. Cover; cook on **LOW 2 hours.**

2. Remove beef from **CROCK-POT**® slow cooker. Shred with two forks. Return beef to sauce; mix well. Serve on rolls.

makes 10 to 12 sandwiches

Tip: Freeze leftovers as individual portions; just reheat in the microwave for fast meals!

Corn on the Cob with Garlic Herb Butter

½ **cups (1 stick) unsalted butter, at room temperature**
3 **to 4 cloves garlic, minced**
2 **tablespoons finely minced fresh parsley**
4 **to 5 ears of corn, husked**
    Salt and black pepper

1. Thoroughly mix butter, garlic and parsley in small bowl.

2. Place each ear of corn on a piece of aluminum foil and generously spread butter mixture on each ear. Season corn with salt and pepper and tightly seal foil.

3. Place corn in 4½-quart slow cooker; overlap ears if necessary. Add enough water to come ¼ of the way up each ear. Cover; cook on **LOW 4 to 5 hours** or **HIGH 2 to 2½ hours** or until done.

makes 4 to 5 servings

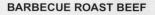
BARBECUE ROAST BEEF

No-Fuss Macaroni and Cheese

2 cups (about 8 ounces) uncooked elbow macaroni

4 ounces light pasteurized processed cheese, cubed

1 cup (4 ounces) shredded mild Cheddar cheese

½ teaspoon salt

⅛ teaspoon black pepper

1½ cups fat-free (skim) milk

Combine macaroni, cheeses, salt and pepper in **CROCK-POT®** slow cooker. Pour milk over all. Cover; cook on **LOW 2 to 3 hours,** stirring after 20 to 30 minutes.

makes 6 to 8 servings

Fresh Herbed Turkey Breast

    2 tablespoons butter, softened

   ¼ **cup fresh sage leaves, minced**

   ¼ **cup fresh tarragon, minced**

    1 clove garlic, minced

    1 teaspoon black pepper

   ½ **teaspoon salt**

    1 (4-pound) split turkey breast

    1 tablespoon plus 1½ teaspoons cornstarch

1. Mix together butter, sage, tarragon, garlic, pepper and salt in small bowl. Rub butter mixture all over turkey breast.

2. Place turkey breast in **CROCK-POT**® slow cooker. Cover; cook on **LOW 8 to 10 hours** or on **HIGH 4 to 5 hours.**

3. Transfer turkey breast to serving platter; cover with foil to keep warm. Slowly whisk cornstarch into cooking juices. Stir into **CROCK-POT**® slow cooker; cook on **HIGH 15 minutes** or until thickened and smooth. Slice turkey breast. Serve with sauce.

makes 8 servings

Tequila-Poached Pears

4 Anjou pears, peeled

2 cups water

1 can (11½ ounces) pear nectar

1 cup tequila

¾ cup sugar

   Juice and peel of 1 lime, plus additional peel for garnish

1. Place pears in **CROCK-POT®** slow cooker.

2. Place remaining ingredients to medium saucepan over medium-high heat; bring to a boil. Boil 1 minute and pour over pears. Cover and cook on **LOW 4 to 6 hours** or on **HIGH 2 to 3 hours** or until pears are tender.

3. Chill and serve on chilled plate drizzled with poaching liquid. Garnish with additional lime peel.

makes 4 servings

Tip: Poaching fruit in a sugar, wine, juice or alcohol syrup helps the fruit retain its shape and adds flavor.

Mushroom Barley Stew

1 tablespoon olive oil
1 medium onion, finely chopped
1 cup chopped carrots (about 2 carrots)
1 clove garlic, minced
1 cup uncooked pearl barley
1 cup dried wild mushrooms, broken into pieces
1 teaspoon salt
½ teaspoon black pepper
½ teaspoon dried thyme
5 cups vegetable broth

1. Heat oil in medium skillet over medium-high heat. Add onion, carrots and garlic; cook and stir 5 minutes or until tender. Place in **CROCK-POT®** slow cooker.

2. Add barley, mushrooms, salt, pepper and thyme. Stir in broth. Cover; cook on **LOW 6 to 7 hours.** Adjust seasonings.

makes 4 to 6 servings

Tip: To turn this thick, robust stew into a soup, add 2 to 3 additional cups of broth. Cook the same length of time.

Simply Delicious Pork

1½ **pounds boneless pork loin, cut into 6 pieces *or*
6 boneless pork loin chops**
4 **medium Golden Delicious apples, cored and sliced**
3 **tablespoons packed light brown sugar**
1 **teaspoon ground cinnamon**
½ **teaspoon salt**

1. Place pork in **CROCK-POT®** slow cooker. Cover with apples.

2. Combine brown sugar, cinnamon and salt in small bowl; sprinkle over apples. Cover; cook on **LOW 6 to 8 hours.**

makes 6 servings

Slow-Roasted Potatoes

16 **small new potatoes**
3 **tablespoons butter, cut into small pieces**
1 **teaspoon paprika**
½ **teaspoon salt**
½ **teaspoon garlic powder**
   Black pepper

Combine all ingredients in **CROCK-POT®** slow cooker; mix well. Cover; cook on **LOW 7 hours** or on **HIGH 4 hours**. Remove potatoes with slotted spoon to serving dish; cover with foil to keep warm. Add 1 to 2 tablespoons water to cooking liquid and stir until well blended. Pour over potatoes.

makes 3 to 4 servings

SIMPLY DELICIOUS PORK

Knockwurst and Cabbage

Olive oil

8 to 10 knockwurst sausages

1 head red cabbage, cut into ¼-inch slices

½ cup thinly sliced white onion

2 teaspoon caraway seeds

1 teaspoon sea salt

4 cups chicken broth

1. Heat oil in skillet over medium heat. Brown knockwursts on all sides, turning as they brown. Transfer to **CROCK-POT®** slow cooker.

2. Add cabbage and onion to **CROCK-POT®** slow cooker. Sprinkle with caraway seeds and salt. Add broth. Cover; cook on **LOW 4 hours** or on **HIGH 2 hours** or until knockwursts are cooked through and cabbage and onions are soft.

makes 8 servings

Bittersweet Chocolate-Espresso Crème Brûlée

  ½ **cup chopped bittersweet chocolate**
  5 **egg yolks**
1¾ **cups whipping cream**
  ¼ **cup brewed espresso**
  ½ **cup granulated sugar**
  ¼ **cup Demerara or raw sugar**

1. Arrange 5 (6-ounce) ramekins or custard cups inside 4½-quart **CROCK-POT®** slow cooker. Pour enough water to come halfway up sides of ramekins (taking care to keep water out of ramekins themselves).

2. Divide chocolate among ramekins.

3. Whisk egg yolks briefly; set aside. Heat cream, espresso and granulated sugar in small saucepan over medium heat, stirring constantly, until mixture begins to boil. Pour hot cream in thin, steady stream into egg yolks, whisking constantly. Pour through fine mesh strainer into clean bowl.

4. Ladle into prepared ramekins in bottom of 4½-quart **CROCK-POT®** slow cooker. Cover and cook on **HIGH 1 to 2 hours** or until custard is set around edges but still soft in centers. Carefully remove and cool to room temperature, then cover and refrigerate until serving.

5. Spread tops of custards with Demerara sugar just before serving; melt with kitchen torch. Serve immediately.

makes 5 servings

Harvest Ham Supper

6 carrots, cut into 2-inch pieces
3 medium sweet potatoes, quartered
1 to 1½ pounds boneless ham
1 cup maple syrup

1. Arrange carrots and potatoes in bottom of **CROCK-POT®** slow cooker to form rack.

2. Place ham on top of vegetables. Pour syrup over ham and vegetables. Cover; cook on **LOW 6 to 8 hours.**

makes 6 servings

Posole

3 pounds boneless pork, cubed
3 cans (14 ounces each) white hominy, drained
1 cup chili sauce
   Cilantro leaves (optional)

Combine all ingredients in **CROCK-POT®** slow cooker. Cover; cook on **HIGH 5 hours**. Reduce temperature to LOW. Cover; cook on **LOW 10 hours.** Garnish with cilantro.

makes 8 servings